Pure Womanhood

Crystalina Evert

Totus Tuus
PRESS
2018

Pure Womanhood
Crystalina Evert
© 2018 Totus Tuus Press, LLC.

Published by Totus Tuus Press, LLC.
P.O. Box 5065
Scottsdale, AZ, 85261
www.totustuuspress.com

Cover by Devin Schadt
Interior by Russell Graphic Design

Printed in the United States of America

978-0-9894905-3-5
978-1-944578-95-4 eBook

I'll never forget the day he walked away from me for the very last time. All I could think was "That guy is leaving with something that never belonged to him in the first place, and I'll never get it back."

I was fifteen, and I knew with all of my heart that it was love. He said that if I loved him, I'd show him. So I did. But before long, he didn't want to spend time with *me* any more; he was spending the time with my body. After that, I began thinking, "Well, I'm not a virgin anymore, so what's the point of waiting for marriage? It's too late for me." After that, one empty relationship led to another as I sought to find the perfect love.

Every woman longs for love, but many of us have gotten hurt and given up on the real thing. We begin to tell ourselves that love doesn't exist or that we don't deserve it. But love does exist and we do deserve it.

So I've named each of the twenty-one sections in this book after one of those excuses, doubts, insecurities, and fears that may be keeping you from the love that God has in mind for you. Maybe you've told yourself all of them, or just a few. But to the extent that you buy into these lies, you'll continue to wonder why love seems so hard to find.

The truth is that your longing for love is there because that's the way God made you. You're meant to have love, He wants you to have love, and He will show you the way to love if you let him.

"Guys don't want the pure girl."

"She's fun for now, but I'd never bring her home to mom and marry her." Ever heard that before? Plenty of guys want the easy girl now, but they plan to settle down with an angel once they're through with their wild stage. So girls feel out of luck either way: Give in to what the guys want, get attention now, and end up discarded or stay pure and fear being alone for the next ten years. Many decide to sit on the fence and find some middle ground, only to end up feeling both used and lonely.

What's the solution?

Twenty-four year-old author Wendy Shalit, recalling the advice of her college friends, wrote:

"You will have many men in your life, they all predicted. Your body's not so bad, your face not so ugly. You'll see, you'll see. You'll do very well on the market. Trust us. Just 'maybe put on a shorter skirt or something,' stop 'hiding' yourself, stop 'taking things so *seriously*,' and 'you'll see how the men will . . .' I tuned out at this point, my mind whirring over this *You will have many men* business. Was that a compliment, I wondered, or a life sentence? It's a life sentence if you're like me, one who hopes for—dare one even say it?—not many men but just one. *You will have many men*. Well, thanks for the generous offer, but am I allowed to decline?"[1]

This woman knew her heart's desire, and she would not settle for less. When it comes to our standards, we will get what we settle for.

So, ask yourself, "Am I a date or a soul mate? Am I a 'for now' girl or a 'forever' girl?" What guy would want a pure girl? Every guy does. The problem is that most young men don't want to be pure. So don't compromise for their sake. Never be afraid that some guy is going to leave you unless you give him something sexual. Let *him* be afraid that he's going to lose *you* unless he knows how to respect you.

"If only I had *her* body."

The lunch bell rang, and we'd flock around our usual table. After the small talk, we'd inevitably discuss food. Rachel had a granola bar and water for breakfast and was splurging with a rice cake for lunch. She carried a notebook that counted every calorie. Ashley bought clothes a few sizes too small to give herself motivation to fit into them. Meanwhile, I had magazine cut-outs of models taped to my bathroom mirror.

No matter how slim we got, we were never satisfied with what we saw in the mirror. It was one thing to have an abusive boyfriend, but it was another thing to have an abusive mind. Like a crow picks at a dead animal, I'd pick at all of my imperfections. All I saw when I looked at myself were the things I wished I could change.

This was life in the popular crowd. We hated our bodies, constantly compared ourselves to others, and walked around school smiling all day. Between all the diet pills and throwing up, we somehow managed to convince ourselves that we were gaining control over our lives and our bodies. The truth is that we were becoming slaves to our insecurities.

The more miserable we became on the inside, the more obsessed—and displeased—we became about the outside. We all thought to ourselves, "If only I could have *her* body, then all of my problems would go away." Because we pinned our self-worth on our looks, our hearts were never at rest.

Why did we put ourselves through this? Why would anyone? Only one thing could motivate someone to such extremes: the desire for love. Why did we never realize that the girl with the most perfect body on campus still didn't have the perfect love?

There came a point when I had to quit blaming my insecurities on guys, magazines, and the media. I had become my own worst enemy. When tempted to put myself down, I had to stop. I had to pray. Instead of comparing myself to everyone, which only causes insecurity, I tried for the first time to see if I actually had any good qualities.

Focusing on my good qualities was harder than I thought it would be. It was not a matter of "just stop thinking about it." Years later, it's still a daily battle. But the difference is that instead of passively harboring insecurities and fueling them, I choose to offer them to God, quit beating myself up, and do something about them. Instead of complaining about my figure, I started kickboxing. Instead of being obsessed about looking perfect in my little outfits, I began to dress modestly and discovered the security that comes with self-respect.

So don't waste your energy and youth destroying yourself. Do something for yourself, for once. While you're at it, find your passion in life, and build up the world and the kingdom of God.

"If he has a bad imagination, that's his problem."

The low-rise jeans, the belly-button shirts, the tight tops. Sure, we enjoyed the feeling of being stared at by the guys, but then we'd get whiny when they were interested in only one thing. We'd complain, but we weren't willing to do anything to fix the problem. After all, our outfits weren't exactly inviting them to improve. All they wanted was what we kept advertising.

Women have power. By the way we dress, by the way we dance, and by the way we carry ourselves, we can invite a man to be a gentleman or a beast. So if a girl wants a guy to appreciate her intelligence and personality, she's probably better off not distracting him with her pierced belly-button.

The question is: "What do I really want? Is it more exciting to be loved by one man or to be gawked at by many?" For those of us who are daring enough to prefer the love of one man, modesty is an unspoken invitation for the guys to be men enough to win our hearts. It's an invitation for the guys to consider that there's so much more about us than just our bodies. That's why modesty is called the guardian of love. Without having to say a word, it sets the standard of respect. But we will never convince a man of our dignity until we first convince ourselves.

Modesty isn't just about the externals, because the way we dress is a sign of the internal. It's telling the world that we don't need to throw ourselves at guys visually in hopes of gaining their attention. Sure, we have the power to turn heads. But we also have the power to turn hearts. We can turn those hearts toward heaven or toward ourselves. But when we turn their attention to our body parts, we're inviting them to "love" us for the wrong thing.

What wins him is what will keep him. If he was won over by a body, it will be the body he stays for (at least until he's bored or loses respect).

We need to rediscover what women have understood for thousands of years: There's a deeper allure in what is *not* seen. To put it simply, purity is beautiful. It crowns natural beauty with mystery. Even after marriage, purity and modesty retain their power to captivate the heart of a man—they just take on a new meaning.

Proverbs 5:17–19 says, "Let your fountain be yours alone, not one shared with strangers; And have joy of the wife of your youth, your lovely hind, your graceful doe. Her love will invigorate you always, through her love you will flourish continually."[2]

When the passage says that the wife's love "invigorates" her husband, the actual Hebrew word can be translated as "intoxicate."[3] God knows the power of a woman's affections, and even the sight of your body takes on a greater mystery when it's "not for strangers."

"Boys will be boys."

I agree. Boys will be boys. But don't you want a man?

If we don't expect more, we'll never get more. When we begin to make excuses for boys, such as "Oh, guys just have needs," we're surrendering our power to improve them. Plain and simple, women teach men how to treat them.

One elderly man said it best: "I've seen a lot of generations come and go, and all the guys have been the same: saying sweet things to get the girls to do stuff with them. But this generation of women is different. They're stupid enough to let the guys have it."

Blunt words, but sadly true.

The fact is that every guy has the ability to be a pure gentleman. But why should he go to the trouble? If he can get all the physical benefits of marriage without even knowing a girl's last name, don't expect him to pop the question anytime soon (much less woo her with real romance). We've taken away a lot of his motivation. All a guy needs to do is give a girl a beer, tell her she's pretty, and the hook-up begins.

We can either keep blaming the guys or do something about it. Instead of male-bashing, we can have the courage to bring out the best in them.

You'd be surprised what guys are capable of when a girl has enough of a backbone to expect to be treated with dignity.

"Good guys don't exist."

Ever since I was a little girl, I dreamed of finding the perfect guy. Sadly, even before I had my driver's permit, I had pretty much called off the search. Instead I put all my energy into maintaining the illusion that my current boyfriend was perfect. I ignored his faults or swept them under the rug. There were all kinds of red flags, but I went ahead anyway, focusing so much on the good that the problems were left in the dark. I wouldn't stand up for myself because I thought it would hurt my chances of keeping this "perfect" guy.

I remember thinking, "When my future husband and I meet, he and I will tell all our stories, and we'll just laugh about it. I'm sure he's out there doing the same stuff I'm doing." Needless to say, I was surprised when I finally met my husband-to-be. He was still a virgin and, at twenty-four, he was still waiting—for me.

It was then that I realized that the bad relationships I had in high school were the natural result of my whole outlook on life. I had a total lack of trust in God. I didn't think He had a plan for girls like me, so I'd grab onto whatever looked like love at the time. All the guys seemed to be interested in the same thing. So, instead of waiting on God, I lowered my standards out of despair and assumed that decent guys were extinct.

When it comes to finding decent guys, perhaps we need to begin by talking about where such men *won't* be found. After a recent talk on purity that my husband gave at a high school, a small group of girls came up to him. One asked what they all wanted to know: Where should we go to find a decent guy?

He began asking about her life. She said she was dating a guy, but he was a drug dealer, drank a lot, swore a lot, and her parents hated him. Her friends chimed in about how bad most guys are and gave an example: "The guys at the parties have been such jerks lately. A couple of weekends ago, they just went up to this one girl and poured a beer on her head. We were all really mad, and then they did it again the next weekend, and again last weekend!" My husband asked them, "What are you doing this weekend?" Their reply? "We're going to a party."

Hmmm.

Let's face it. Women long for the love, approval, and acceptance of men. Men long for the same from women. Just look at the cover of any men's or women's magazine with their offers of "436 ways to allure the opposite sex."

Those magazines probably aren't offering any good advice, but they're onto something. It's the way God made us, male and female, to be a gift for each other.

Some women who think of themselves as "independent" and "liberated" deny that they need male approval. They see it as a weakness. Perhaps because they've seen men take advantage of women, they confuse the vulnerability of being open to love with weakness. In reality, it takes strength, wisdom, trust, and courage to be open to the risks of love. It's not weakness to desire love. The weakness is when we settle for less than love.

We also need to remember than no man can fill our longing for acceptance completely. Ultimately, that can be fulfilled only by God, whose deep love for us should be shown to us through our parents and especially, in the case of God the Father, through our dads. Unfortunately, when that doesn't happen, we often try to build up our self-worth through relationships with guys. Instead of looking to the Heavenly Father, we look to boyfriends to fill that void. But the Bible tells us, "Even if my father and mother forsake me, the Lord will take me in" (Ps. 27:10, NAB).

I'm sure you've seen those glittery t-shirts or bumper stickers that say "Princess." It's as if we all have this longing to be adored and cherished like one. That desire to be cherished is written on our hearts, because our Heavenly Father is the King, and the daughter of the King is truly a princess.

I had heard all that before, but it never sunk in because I wasn't praying. When I finally let God love me as I was, I began to know the dignity and respect I deserved as a daughter of the King.

It may take a while for that to sink in, but when it does, your relationships with guys will be a *reflection* of the Father's love instead of a *replacement* for it. In the mean time, if you want to meet a good guy, get involved in things that good guys do. Better yet, *instead of looking for the ideal man, become the ideal woman and let him look for you.* Keep your eyes on God and know that when it comes to finding a decent guy, the patient girl gets the prize.

"As long as I stay a virgin . . ."

"Okay, I'll do *this* with him, but I won't do *that.*" All of my biggest mistakes began with little compromises. "I'll still be a virgin, so it won't be that big of a deal." Then a little further. Then the big talk: "I think we went a little too far." "Yeah, we need to make sure we don't do that again." Of course, that boundary doesn't last long, and sooner or later old boundaries turn into stepping stones toward sex.

Before long, there's nothing left but sex. Because of everything that's happened already, turning back doesn't seem like an option. That's when the rationalization begins: "It's not that big of a deal. Everybody's doing it. We'll stay together. This is love."

One clue that you're doing something wrong is when you start spending a lot of time trying to convince yourself that what you're doing is right. That's a sign that your conscience is bothering you.

God made our hearts for love, so love brings peace. But lust brings stress. All at once, we think, "I know I shouldn't be doing this, but how do I stop? Well, it will just be this time."

There is no peace until there is total love. I lived with a constant, inescapable fear of getting pregnant, getting caught, getting infected, and getting used. Sometimes the fear was overwhelming, and at other times it was the tiniest whisper in the back of my mind. But it was always there. I began to numb my conscience and value the gift of my body less and less. Over time, those little compromises led to the loss of my virginity. It was only a matter of time, considering the people with whom I chose to spend my time.

In my circle of friends, virginity was seen as an embarrassing lack of experience. It made you feel like a prude or someone who couldn't find a date. It was practically a curse. Not once do I remember hearing that virginity is the most beautiful gift you could give your husband. Losing it was seen as an accomplishment, a rite of passage into womanhood and real life. Sadly, some of my friends thought of it as something "you just need to get over with."

We made fun of virgins in public, but I secretly respected and admired them, wishing I was in their place. At any point they could become like me, but I could never regain what they had. Once you give it away, everything changes. You feel like a piece of you died, and what you once hoped was love becomes distorted. Everyone talks about how hard it is to say no, but no one tells you how hard it is when you say yes.

So, what should our standard be as women? To love and respect yourself, glorify God with your body, and avoid doing anything with a guy that you would not want some girl doing with your future husband.

When it comes to drawing the line, understand that boundaries that get set over and over again are not really boundaries. Purity is a challenge for every couple, but there's a huge difference between striving for purity and being dominated by lust. Only when *both* people see purity as the goal can they be free to build a relationship based on true love with God as the center. When two people don't share this goal, one will often pressure the other. Sometimes the pressure is obvious. More often, it is subtle: The guy doesn't aggressively push boundaries; he just acts sweet and takes everything sexual she's willing to give him.

What many girls don't realize is that once a guy is sexually aroused, his desires aren't satisfied until he tries everything. Then, once he's tried every*thing* with one girl, he's still not satisfied, and he wants to try every*one*. Girls sometimes allow this (or even initiate it) out of a desire to feel closer to him. But the closeness lasts only as long as the pleasure.

That's why purity shows integrity. You're not arousing the guy and then slamming on the brakes. Instead, you're inviting him to love. If he runs from the challenge, then you're better off without him.

"I'm not going to have sex until I'm ready."

I figured that if he could hold out without sex for six months, then he loved me. Now I look back and think, "Six months is the price I put on my body? Six months of his time, attention, and phone calls—that's the definition of love?"

In deciding not to have sex until we're "ready" or until we're "truly in love," what's really happening is that we're trying to determine the time for sex based upon the intensity of our emotions. Sure, we might feel ready in six months, but where's he going to be in twelve months? If we say we won't have sex until we meet the "right guy," what we're thinking is that the only mistake would be sleeping with the *wrong* guy.

Standards based upon emotions don't come with clear guidelines, and vague standards get worn down easily. But if the standard is "sex is for marriage," there's no debating when marriage takes place: Either he's your husband or he's not.

If a man loves a woman, he will wait for her. Not only that, he will wait *with* her, because he has the same values and will focus on guarding her purity as well as his own. But be careful. Some guys act like they're fine with the chastity thing, but in three weeks they're trying the same old stuff. That's when you have to have the guts to get out. Not only does such a guy not deserve your body—he doesn't even deserve your time.

However, guarding your purity is only half the battle. All too often women have no boundaries with their emotions. What I mean is that we often give our hearts away so quickly that we're emotionally married to the guy after a few months. All the talk of being together forever not only makes physical purity more difficult, but it makes breakups feel more like divorces.

Sometimes diving in too deep too fast is a sign of a lack of deep relationships with others. Sometimes it's a sign of a desperate desire for love. The solution is to focus on developing stronger relationships with the people in your life who truly love you and, in the meantime, to guard your heart.

It's one thing to save your body for your husband, and it's another to save your heart for him, too. One man said, "If I'm interested in a girl, it may be frustrating if she doesn't fall for me right away, but deep down I am all the more intrigued by the challenge of winning her heart."[4]

Guarding your heart doesn't mean building walls around it; it means having the confidence to take the time to let love blossom. As the love song from the Bible says, "Do not arouse, do not stir up love before its own time" (Song 3:5, NAB).

"If I say no, I might lose him."

A recent poll of high school sex-ed classes asked girls what their number one question on sexuality was. Contrary to the teachers' expectations, it wasn't about birth control or sexually transmitted diseases. The girls wanted to know how to say no to a guy without hurting his feelings. Sure, they didn't want to hurt his feelings, but veiled under this is a more secret concern: They feared his rejection.

I know the feeling. I remember giving in to a boy-friend's pressure because if I resisted, we'd get in a fight. Everything in my heart said no. I knew sometimes he saw me as something to be conquered, but I tried not to think about it. I figured, "Well, I love him, and this keeps him happy. It's not like we haven't done it before. Besides, I don't want to break up after giving him so much."

I think one girl put it well when she said, "I felt strange and, in a sense, used. It was like we were both caring for the same person—him. I felt left out of it."[5]

Feeling that way was a clear signal to dump him, but I didn't. I felt like I couldn't. I was scared to death that if I left him, I'd miss out on love. I couldn't see that I was already missing out on love by staying with someone who loved sex more then he loved me.

A girl knows she's being used when she distracts herself and rationalizes everything. She becomes so busy focusing on what she's *not* doing that she never realizes what she *is* doing. She's afraid to say no and draw the line, because that would be a test of his love, and she knows he'll fail the test. Deep down, she's afraid that he likes her only for the pleasure she gives him. So, she just goes along, meeting his "needs" and dreaming that things will change.

But *purity never ruins loving relationships.* If the relationship is based on lust, purity will end it. But if the relationship is based on love, purity will save it. One high school girl said, "Since my boyfriend and I stepped back I've gained so much more respect for him. We've grown closer, we respect each other more, we know we're doing what God wants, we've grown in our love, and we have so much more fun when we're together. And it's all because we got rid of the stress of all the physical things."

Purity is love. In the words of another young woman: "My love for him is so strong that I don't want to compromise his dignity. I intend to become his wife!"

Girls who are serious about finding love need to get a backbone, like these women. Imagine if every woman on earth began to be pure and respect her body and her future husband. Sure, plenty wouldn't have dates next weekend, but the guys would figure out pretty quickly that if they want female company, they have to be gentlemen.

By valuing her own purity, the girl can help the guy understand that her body is a treasure to be cherished, not some goal to be conquered.

When it comes to saying no, refusal skills don't start when you're already being physically intimate with a guy and he wants to try something new. Saying no means not putting yourself in that situation in the first place. It might even start with saying no to dating that guy at all. You have to start by saying no bad relation-ships and meaningless hook-ups before they begin.

When a relationship begins the right way—with a long, God-centered friendship—there probably won't be any need to tell the guy no: He will be enough of a man of God to lead you to purity. Finding a man like this is not a ridiculous dream. It's a standard.

If a guy keeps trying to do sexual stuff after the girl says no, and she doesn't break up with him, she's teaching him to disrespect her. After all, if she has to give a guy something sexual to keep him, she's going to lose him anyway, because he doesn't really love her. He's just trying to get what he wants by wearing down her commitment with his charm, guilt, anger, threats, affection—whatever.

If he really loves you, he won't pressure you.

I know one teenage girl who took sex out of her relationship. Now her boyfriend buys her a white rose at the beginning of each month as a sign of their new commitment.

Don't you want a man like this? If you're settling for less, quit feeling sorry for yourself and get out. If you're still afraid to say no, step back and realize what a bad sign that is. What does that say about him and what he's after?

You don't have to wait until you "have great self-esteem" before you start saying no, because it is by saying no that you will get that self-respect. Earn it. If you constantly worry that a guy will reject you unless you give him something sexual, you're missing the chance to invite him to become a man. It is here, where you think you're the weakest, that you really have the most power.

"Older guys are more mature."

Someone recently told me she overheard a guy say, "We already got all the seniors and juniors. Let's go de-virginize the freshmen and sophomores." Granted, not all older guys are like this. But plenty of them are. He'll flatter a girl with his attention, and while she's busy thinking how "nice" he is, he's slowly wearing down her innocence.

The girl thinks she's really special for dating such a mature guy, and she probably won't have the self-esteem to turn down his sexual advances. She may even feel she owes it to him because he's willing to date her. She usually ends up getting burned because she's trying to find the love and approval that her dad never gave her.

Looking back, I see that the absence of a father in my life made me more vulnerable to dating older guys, because I longed for the security, protection, and affection that I thought they could offer. But if they had been as mature as I thought they were, they probably would have been dating girls their own ages.

Think about it: As a senior, would you bring a freshman boy to prom? Most girls would laugh at the idea, but we feel flattered when the tables are turned. The same goes for college guys chasing high school girls. When you're in college, do you plan on pursuing high school boys?

"I'll change him."

Kristen proudly displayed for us her newest diamond promise ring from Nick. Nick and Kristen were attached at the hip and seemed practically married in high school. I knew he had cheated on her twice already and I thought, "What an idiot she is." Then I looked down at the promise ring on my hand and thought, "What an idiot I am."

We were both in disastrous relationships, but we stayed put. Maybe we stayed because if we left we would have to admit the huge mistakes we had made with the guys. Maybe we stayed out of pity, thinking we could rescue them from their problems. Maybe we were really in love with someone who existed only in our imaginations. Maybe it was all of these things, fueled by our longing to be desired by someone.

Whatever the reason, we played the hero and got played. We didn't end up fixing either guy, but we both needed a lot of healing when it was all over. We confused their physical affection for love and pretended to ourselves that their possessiveness was a sign of fidelity. In reality, a guy who tries to control a girl is a guy who is insecure. He's just trying to get control of his own life at the girl's expense. The longer I stayed in denial and dragged it on, the deeper the wounds became.

It seemed as if the more sexual we became with them, the less satisfied we were. We always complained that guys use girls for sexual stuff, but we were just as guilty for using the sexual stuff as a way to control and keep the guys. We could use it to win his attention, get back at him, or mend our hurting self-esteem. When that backfired and sex didn't keep him or empower us, we were left blaming ourselves. We looked for self worth in the arms of guys and were left feeling like a discarded showpiece.

Through it all, I discovered that you should never commit to a guy—whether it is in dating or in marriage—hoping that he will change. Commit to a guy only if you like him exactly as he is. Otherwise, you're committing to an imaginary man.

Many women drag bad relationships on for years, afraid of what the guy will do to himself if she's not there to rescue him. If a guy turns to drinking, drugs, or other destructive behavior to cope with life's difficulties, it's not your fault. It isn't your job to protect him from himself. After all, how is he supposed to take care of you if he can't take care of himself?

"He won't do it again."

"I'm sorry, honey. You're the one I really love. I don't know what I was thinking." He knew everything to say to get her back: He'd turn on the guilt, remind her of the good times, and act all sad. And it worked. My friend Alicia caught her boyfriend cheating on her, and she was sleeping with him again that same night. Just as he used his charm to manipulate her insecurities to win her back, she used the power of sex as a way to regain her place. Needless to say, eventually he was gone.

What a huge price she paid. And for what? Her image? Emotional "security"? It was for nothing. Holding onto him was like holding onto sand slipping through her fingers. She made a thousand excuses in her mind about why he wouldn't answer his cell phone or why his stories weren't straight about what he and the guys did on Saturday nights. When she asked him about it, he'd make her think that she was crazy, and then he'd change the subject by questioning *her* faithfulness.

Many girls date players and try to please them to win their respect. But the girls never get respected. Men respect women who are not afraid to have standards. When a girl doesn't have standards, she clings to an unfaithful guy and justifies it by saying, "I'm a really forgiving person" or "I just like to make him happy."

What she's really doing is giving a guy sexual stuff so she can have someone around for Valentine's Day.

When a girl is desperate, she assumes that having a cheater is better than having no guy at all. It's so sad, because God wants women to have something so much better. If we won't trust him, we miss out.

We've all heard friends say, "Stay away from him. He's a total player, and he's only after one thing." The girl responds with "You're just jealous that he likes me and not you." She thinks, "They'll see. I'm different from those other girls in his past."

We have to let go of our insecurities, foolishness, and pride and pray for wisdom.

It's easy to know when a friend should end a relationship. But it's tough when you're that girl. How do you know when to let go of *your* guy? Here's a reliable "dump him" list:

- You've had to tell him more than once to stop.
- You feel the need to fix him.
- He looks at pornography.
- He hits you, pushes you, or does anything to frighten you.
- He gets drunk or takes drugs.
- He doesn't care if you lie to your family.
- He leads you away from God.
- He puts you down (even if he then says he's "just

kidding").

- He cheats on you.
- He's controlling.
- He lies to you.
- He flirts with other girls.
- He uses guilt to get you to do what he wants.
- He always resents time you spend with your friends and family.
- He keeps you from fulfilling your goals and dreams.
- He behaves badly and then blames it on other people or on things that happen to him.
- He can't stand on his own two feet without you.
- You can't stand on your own two feet and remain pure with him.

These are not minor faults. They are signs of major issues than can be disastrous to a future marriage. If any *one* of these applies to him, end the relationship *now*.

One way is to call him when you have a friend by your side for support. Another way is to write a long letter. A letter allows you to make sure he knows your reasons. If he forgets any, he can always refer back to the letter. He may try to manipulate you to stay, but you must be firm. Think of all the times you should have been firm with him, and make up for all of them in one letter.

In the mean time, stay strong. Do nothing physical with him. No kissing. No holding hands. No nothing.

This man is not your husband, and your affections do not belong to him. Any affection you show him is leading him on. If the idea of breaking up terrifies you, at least step away from the relationship for a few weeks to "detox" from it and clear your mind. Cut off all contact with him, and cling to God, good friends, and family. Hopefully after this break, you'll have more confidence in your decision to leave. You are worth it.

"I can't be alone."

"We've been through so much, and we've made it this far. I don't want to leave him."

We had broken up more times than I could count, but we always ended up falling back into the relationship. We were indecisive and confused. It was obvious that neither of us was free.

Only a person who is free can give the gift of love. Just as some guys are enslaved by their hormones, I was enslaved by my fear of being alone. I felt alone while I was with him, so I didn't want to imagine how lonely I would feel without him. *But putting up with just about anything to avoid facing your fears isn't love.*

While men usually determine their sense of worth by their accomplishments, women usually measure their sense of worth by the quality of their relationships. If their relationships are bad, they're feeling bad. That isn't to say that men aren't affected by their relationships, but generally they're more detached.

What this means for women is that we're more likely to form intimate bonds with people, and we therefore run the risk of determining our worth by them. We may jump into relationships for shallow reasons instead of taking our time to look for the qualities we want in a future husband. Our lives can become teenage soap operas, like my life became. I lost friends for the sake of passing guys.

As much as we might hate the idea of being single, sometimes the thing we fear most is what we need most. Not only *can* we be single, but sometimes we *should* be. If we want to find love, we need to get to know ourselves before we get to know anyone else. Otherwise, we may try to find our identities in guys.

Being single has a purpose. It frees us to set our goals and dreams in life so that we know what our passions are and how we want to improve the world. It opens our eyes. Being single does not mean being alone; being single means having an opportunity to learn to live for others. Don't be afraid to take time off from the relationship scene. The truth is that being independent makes us more attractive.

It's easy when you're lonely to buy into the lie that no one else is lonely. But I guarantee that some of the most popular people at your school are lonelier than anyone would imagine. Everyone thought my circle of friends was happy, but they never knew about the drugs, the eating disorders, the diet pills, the drinking problems, the broken families, the lack of acceptance, and the cheating boyfriends.

If you feel lonely, turn to God and "cast all your anxieties on him, for He cares about you" (1 Pet. 5:7). Trust God with your heart and with your body. It is only when you are satisfied with his love that you will be able to accept the love He has planned for you.

"Parents are clueless."

I thought I was fooling my mom, but I was fooling only myself. For years, I did things my way and told more lies than I could count. My lifestyle showed that I valued the opinion of guys more than that of my family—as if this guy I had known for six months loved me more than my own flesh and blood.

In a way, I wanted my mom to know what was going on, but I didn't want to tell her. I was scared to death that I'd get grounded until I was forty. More importantly, I was terrified of what she'd think of me.

Of course, my mom knew how I was living. She wanted something so much better for me, but every time she tried to help me, I thought she was trying to control me and take something away.

If you want to change your parents' opinion of a guy, all you should have to do is be honest about him.

If he's a gentleman of character, purity, faithfulness, and honesty, those qualities will become obvious. Instead of wrestling with your parents about him, try to see why they don't like him. Maybe you know exactly why they don't like him but are ignoring it. You refuse to see it as a problem, and you think you'll be able to change him.

If you're lying to your family and sneaking around, don't expect your boyfriend to win the respect of your family. Lying to them and going against their will only creates resentment.

Any relationship divorced from your family's influence and direction is an unhealthy relationship. Therefore, the sooner you get a real relationship with your parents, the better. God promises that if we honor our parents, good will come of it. It was eerie how soon my relationships began to improve after I realized that. Sure, that's easier said than done, and I know not everyone's family is perfect, but you have to start somewhere. If you have trouble talking face-to-face with your parents, consider writing them a letter to express your hopes, hurts, apologies, or whatever needs to be said, to begin the conversation. If your parents don't offer you guidance, find some adult you trust and seek advice there.

In the meantime, make smart choices with guys. Especially if you come from a broken family, know that the decisions you make now about guys will determine whether one day you can give your kids the family peace you never had.

"It's all fun and games."

I can still smell the stench of pot and beer that hit us as we walked into each party. The smell was always the same, as was the sound of pounding music that filled the houses. The guys were the same. The girls were the same. The conversations the next day were the same: "Oh my gosh, I was sooo drunk."

At first, it was cool just to be at the parties. When we didn't feel accepted by others, our families, or even ourselves, the environment brought a feeling of almost immediate acceptance. The problem was that we weren't sober enough to know who we were accepting. I think that's what made it so appealing. If someone accepts you with a mask on, at least you feel accepted. Who knows if they'd like you without the mask?

One night, I decided not to drink but sit back and watch everything. From the outside looking in, the music was hypnotizing. The whole environment was so dark—maybe because none of us really wanted to see what we chose to surround ourselves with. The guys and girls were hanging all over each other. One new couple was sharing an intimate moment in the backyard on a lawn chair in front of everyone. The people dancing were basically having sex with their clothes on, and I heard conversations like "I love you so much. It's so great to see you!" But the guy was so drunk that he was probably seeing three of her. Except for the occasional fistfights, everyone looked really happy. I watched a guy approach a girl, stare at her like a piece of meat, and tell her some degrading sexual joke. She giggled and flirted, eating up the attention.

It struck me: How desperate are we? In the parable of the prodigal son, the son who left home longed to eat his fill of pig food. Well, here we were, doing the same thing: being degraded and taking it as flattery. What I used to find so alluring suddenly filled me with disgust. It was all fake. With a drink in hand, we were trying to convince everyone that we were happy so that maybe we would believe it ourselves.

We said it was all fun and games, but when morning came the fun and games were over, and the drama began: "What was I thinking?" We knew all along what stupid things we did, but we drank to cover the shame and then we blamed the alcohol as a pathetic way to say it wasn't our fault. Then we went back to the party to numb the pain of an unhappy life, and the cycle went on.

"This time it will be different."

"Like a dog that returns to his vomit is a fool that repeats his folly" (Prov. 26:11). It's not a lovely image, but it fit me perfectly. I did the same things over and over, trying to convince myself that "next time, it will be better. It's not a big deal." What's not a big deal? My body? My heart? I knew it was a huge deal, but I thought I was the only one not satisfied, so I kept trying.

Unfortunately, you can't hide from yourself when you're all alone. When I went to bed at night, I knew I was living a lie. We all lied to our parents, but it took me a while before I realized that I was lying to myself. I walked into the party and left my dignity at the door. Actually, I left my dignity at home when I decided to go the party, because I knew what was waiting for me. At first, I struggled with this, thinking, "Well, I can just go to the party and not drink. I can set an example." What an example that would be: A Christian girl who needs to surround herself with drunk friends because she fears being alone. What an inspiration! I'm sure they'll all convert.

I wasn't going there for their sake. I spent time and effort getting ready and plotting lies to my family to get the attention of boys I knew I never wanted to marry. Why did I care so much about what drunk guys thought about me, anyway? Why should I destroy myself for the sake of their company?

Sure, I hated it. But I thought, "I'm a teen. This is just how it's supposed to be." My excuse was that I saw no other option. I figured, "Am I supposed to sit at home every Saturday night?" I didn't want to lose my friends. I didn't want to be lonelier than I already was. What I didn't want to admit was that even my "best" friends weren't friends. But I had no one to blame. No one was choosing that lifestyle for me.

There was a tug-of-war going on in my conscience. I wanted my self-respect back, but I was scared of the price I would pay. One night, I captured all these thoughts in a letter to whoever would be my future husband:

Beloved,
It's Friday night, my so-called friends have just left, and I feel incredibly alone! You see, they all came over in their little skirts and tight shirts, wanting me to go clubbing. It was a normal Friday-night thing to do. They were drinking and tried so hard to convince me to go, and it was very tempting. I felt pulled in two separate directions, and part of me did want to go. But my other half knew what was waiting for me there. I couldn't. As they left my house frustrated, I could hear them saying, "What? She thinks she's too good for us now?" I'm slowly starting to feel like a stranger to my friends. Is all this trouble, tears, and sadness worth it in the long run? Do I really know what I'm doing? I know there is something better than this, and I'm trying to see that. But at times like this, it's hard. I'm praying for

you. Know I give all this to you.
Giving you all my love,
Crystalina

"Nobody's getting hurt."

Could there be a bigger lie that we feed ourselves? I said it a million times. I knew I was getting hurt, but I played it off and acted invincible. Even as I said it, I thought of the tears I was shedding behind closed doors. I tried to ignore the hurt it would cause to myself, my family, and my future husband. I didn't even want to think about God and what He felt watching His daughter slowly destroying herself.

We know the spiritual and emotional harm we cause ourselves, but what about physical harm? The truth is that our bodies, like our hearts, are not made for multiple sexual partners. We're made for enduring love.

Here's why:

- The more sexual partners a woman has, the more likely she is to get cervical cancer. This is caused by the most commonly transmitted STD, human papillomavirus (HPV). However, condoms offer minimal protection against the virus because it is spread from mid-thigh to mid-abdomen contact.[6] Any skin-to-skin sexual contact in that region, including hand-to-genital contact, can transmit it.[7] How common is the virus? *The Journal of the American Medical Association* reported that 40 percent of sexually active teenage girls are currently infected with HPV.[8]

- Chlamydia can rob a woman of her ability to have kids. Just as hormonal birth control increases a woman's chances of getting certain STDs, being on the shot (Depo-Provera) triples your chances of being infected with Chlamydia, because it interferes with your immune system.[9] The National Institutes of Health admits that condoms do not guarantee prevention of chlamydia.[10]

- A woman infected with herpes will have it for the rest of her life and can pass it on to her husband and children. Because condom use only decreases the risk of herpes transmission by about fifty percent,[11] the American College of Obstetricians and Gynecologists reports that "the use of a condom doesn't provide reliable protection against herpes."[12]

- Eight out of ten people who have an STD don't know that they're infected.[13] One study showed that three-fourths of men who knew they had an STD admitted to sleeping with women without telling them about the infection.[14]

So why do they teach us the myth of "safe sex"? They put us on birth control because they think we're incapable of self-control.

"It's my body. It's my choice."

I remember sitting alone in the bathroom, waiting with anguish to see if I was pregnant. The sixty seconds seemed like an eternity. "Negative! Thank God!"

Eight years later, and recently married, my husband and I flipped over the test, saw that it was positive, and cried for joy. What a difference the sacrament of marriage makes.

In high school, taking pregnancy tests scared me to death. The experience would freak me out for a while, but then I'd be back to the same old ways. Out of fear, I went on the birth control pill and later took the shot. But something happened in me each time I popped a pill or took the shot. I felt like part of me was dying. I suppose that when we disrespect our bodies in a relationship, we become careless with our bodies in other ways. We even begin to act against our bodies. It's like we start to separate ourselves from our bodies.

Here I am, sixteen years old and perfectly healthy but taking drugs to make me sexually available. The drugs made me nauseous, moody, depressed, and bloated. I remember asking myself again and again, "Why am I putting myself through this?" I knew it wasn't for me, but I still had no answer. There was just confusion and darkness. My boyfriend wasn't much help, saying, "Oh, just try it a little longer. It'll be okay." In other words, "I don't care if you hurt your body. If I can have sex without responsibility, life is great." The birth control companies tell you it's liberating, but "enslaving" would be a better description.

Contraception not only turns you against your own body, but it often causes resentment toward men in general. Have you ever heard an angry girl say, "Guys have no clue what it's like to be sixteen and have to flip over a pregnancy test"? It's true: Guys would probably act differently about sex if they were the ones who could get pregnant.

On the other hand, no man will ever know what it's like for his body to become a tabernacle of life. A woman's fertility is a gift, not a curse. MTV, Planned Parenthood, and *Cosmo* would have us believe that pregnancy is some kind of disease. They endlessly promote shots, patches, and pills to spay us.

They never tell us the whole truth about birth control: the increased risk of breast cancer,[15] that the pill and the shot often cause abortions when the baby is only about a week old without the mom ever knowing it.[16] They often tell us we need the pill for medical reasons without telling us that there are usually other alternatives.[17]

Often, birth control "fails" for whatever reason, and the woman finds herself pregnant and feeling helpless and alone. But even if you're pregnant and unmarried, pregnancy is always a gift. Although it may seem frightening now, know that God has a reason for everything. If you feel afraid and alone, and don't know what to do, call a local crisis pregnancy center. (Call 1-800-712-4357 or text "HELPLINE" to 313131.) They'll help you to make the choice that you can live with.

Sadly, many young women are encouraged by society to take the life of the baby as a quick fix. The clinic may say they're just removing tissue so that you can go back to life as normal. But where will they be three years from now when the baby's (would-be) birthday rolls around and you're bawling because he's not there?

If you're on the pill for birth control, get off and use self-control instead. If you're already pregnant, get help and guard the life of your baby, no matter what anyone says. If you've already suffered through an abortion, God offers you an ocean of mercy. Go to Him in prayer and in the sacrament of reconciliation. Get in touch with a post-abortion healing program such as Project Rachel at 800-5-WECARE, where you can talk to someone who understands what you've been through.

From today on, decide to live a pure life. By being pure, you're loving your body, you're loving your future children, you're loving your future husband, and, most importantly, you're loving your God.

"I'm damaged goods."

One in three girls is sexually abused by the time she's eighteen years old.[18] These young women often feel totally alone. Maybe it was a family member, a brother's friend, or a total stranger. Whoever it was, physical or emotional abuse leaves unseen wounds that take years to heal. Especially when the abuse is sexual, it can cause a deep distrust and resentment of the opposite sex. Sometimes, it can even create a perceived need for the opposite sex.

All too often, out of fear or shame, the victim keeps the incident a secret. Sexual abusers thrive off this silence. That's why they often use seduction instead of force: so the victim will think she was willing to be taken advantage of.

She may attempt to sweep the memories under the rug, hoping that they'll just go away. She may harbor a fear that if people knew what happened, they would look down on her and treat her like damaged goods. She may even blame herself or begin to harm her body to numb the emotional pain. Because of the hurt, she may turn from God and doubt His love. She may conclude that she's unlovable. This is the most dangerous point, because she may open herself up to unhealthy relationships out of a feeling of despair that she doesn't deserve anything better.

If you have been abused, be assured that although you can't change the past, you can keep the past from determining you future. You are not alone. Try to find an adult you trust and talk about it.

It's understandable that life's tragedies cause us to doubt God. But even if your faith seems gone, and love seems impossible, do not let go of hope. Pope John Paul II said to young people, "Your hearts bear so many wounds, often caused by the adult world!"[19] The Holy Father said He had lived through much darkness, but "I have seen enough evidence to be unshakably convinced that no difficulty, no fear is so great that it can completely suffocate the hope that springs eternal in the hearts of the young. Do not let that hope die! Stake your lives on it! We are not the sum of our weaknesses and failures; we are the sum of the Father's love for us."[20]

So do not think that you are worthless or worth *less* because of the past. No matter what has happened, you still have yourself to give. You are still God's unique creation, made *by* love and *for* love—the love God intended you to have when He created you in your mother's womb. If you're called to marriage, then by giving yourself fully to God, you will one day be able to give yourself fully to your husband when you marry.

"It's too late for me."

Once it's gone, it's gone. That's all that ran though my head, because I knew I could never get my virginity back. One bad relationship led to another, and with each breakup came a deeper despair. After a few years of this, I was tired of running from reality and hiding from the truth. I was sick of never having any peace.

It is said that if a lamb constantly veers away from the safety of the flock and into danger, the shepherd will break its legs and then carry it on his shoulders and personally care for it. By the time the bones mend and the lamb can walk again, it has come to love and trust the shepherd so much that it never leaves his side. I felt just as broken as that lamb, having tried time and time again to run away from God to find the love that only He could give me. For my own sake, He let me hit rock bottom.

His words "Apart from me you can do nothing" (John 15:5) had never been clearer to me. Until then, I thought that without a guy I could do nothing. But I realized that no man's affections can replace the security of knowing the love of God.

Time and time again I said it was "too late for me," but I realized that was a cop-out, an excuse to avoid the challenging task of restoring my self-respect. My laziness and pride were the real things holding me back.

It also showed that I hadn't forgiven myself. But everyone in the world has things in their past that they wish they could erase. Those who live great lives are the ones who learn from the mistakes instead of repeating them and letting themselves be defeated by them.

So have some confidence in yourself and some faith in God. The regrets about your past may seem overwhelming, but God's love is greater. To help you heal and start over, visit my website womenmadenew.com.

"What good guy would want me?"

Dirty. If there was one word that captured what I feared people would think of me, that was it. When I met my future husband and learned that he was still a virgin, all of the doubts in the world taunted me: "No way would he want to spend the rest of his life with someone like me. If he only knew everything that I did years before, he'd run from me."

But he didn't. The day I told him about my past was one of the hardest days of my life. It was only then, as I looked into his forgiving eyes, that I realized the magnitude of what I had given away. Tears still came from time to time, but I learned that living purity is truly healing and that God is never outdone in generosity. Now, the way my husband looks at me is a reminder that Jesus' promise is true: "Behold, I make all things new" (Rev. 21:5).

Through all of my bad relationships, I knew deep down that God wanted something different for me. But I wouldn't trust him. I longed for love, but part of me said to forget that fairy tale: "Give it up. There aren't any good guys out there. And even if there were, they wouldn't want you." It's ironic that one minute we're saying that no guy would want a pure girl, and the next minute we're saying that no guy would want us because we're not pure.

So, what good guy would want you? For starters, Jesus does. With him, there is no fear that He doesn't love you. While most girls are called to the married life, our hearts should also be open to hear the call to be the Bride of Christ in the religious life. We all desire a spousal love, and He is one spouse who will always welcome us.

God's plans for us are infinitely greater than anything we could dream of. It doesn't matter what we've done. All that matters is where we go from here. As Mother Teresa said, "He loves you, but even more, He longs for you. He misses you when you don't come close. He thirsts for you. He loves you always, even when you don't feel worthy. When not accepted by others, even by yourself sometimes, He is the one who always accepts you. Only believe that you are precious to him. Bring all you are suffering to His feet, only open your heart to be loved by Him as you are. He will do the rest."[21]

"It's impossible to stay pure."

I rarely prayed, surrounded myself with the wrong friends, dated players, and was shocked at how hard it was to be pure. If we seriously desire to be pure, we need to realize that it's not the absence of sex that makes us pure. It's the daily desire to glorify God with our bodies.

So if you've tried a different lifestyle in the past, and you're ready for something new, try chastity. Take on the mindset of one high school girl, who said, "Yes, attention from boys feels good, but knowing that I'm too good for most of them feels even better."

It's a lifestyle that guides everything from the way we dress to the way we dance to the places we go on Friday nights. It's living with purpose instead of being passive and constantly surprised or disappointed that we can't find love. Sure, the lifestyle is difficult. But the sacrifices we make now train us for the sacrifices that can hold a marriage together. Furthermore, the challenge of purity builds in us the character and class that good men look for in a bride. But ultimately, we should not practice chastity in order to become more appealing to virtuous men, but rather to please God. By making God our focus rather than man, we purify our intentions as well as our souls.

When God calls us to live a certain way, He gives us the means to do it. So, Jesus left us the sacraments of reconciliation and the Eucharist. I went through the motions of learning about them from church or school, but to me they seemed like burdensome requirements or boring rituals. As for confession, it scared me to death, so I avoided it like the plague. But I was only running from mercy.

I whined that it was hard to be pure while refusing to use the best two supports that God had given me. It was only with the power of the Mass and the graces that come from confession that I was able to start over without turning back. Following confession, I had a peace that no relationship ever seemed to offer. Instead of being an occasion for embarrassment, the sacrament became an experience of joy. I began to deepen my prayer life, and I took up a special devotion to the Blessed Virgin Mary, God's idea of the perfect woman.

One man said of Mary: "She is the one whom every man loves when he loves a woman—whether he knows it or not. She is what every woman wants to be when she looks at herself. She is the woman whom every man marries in ideal when he takes a spouse; she is the secret desire every woman has to be honored and fostered; she is the way every woman wants to command respect and love because of the beauty of her goodness of body and soul."[22]

Sure enough, after I got married, my husband gave me a letter he had written as a teen to whoever would be his future wife. In it, he said he longed for the day he would meet her and that he hoped she would be a woman with a love for the Virgin Mary.

Not only has Mary given us Jesus, but Jesus has

given His Mother, Mary, to *us* to be *our* Mother. There is no fear, depth of loneliness, or longing that she has not experienced. Mary understands our needs as young women since she was one, and she stands ready to help us.

If you've never had any special devotion to Mary, begin by asking her to intercede for you in obtaining the grace of purity. With grace, you will see that a pure life is not the life of a prude. It's the life of a pure woman, in love with her God and full of hope.

As daughters of the King of heaven, may our one desire be the same as St. Faustina: "From today onward, I am going to strive for the greatest purity of soul, that the rays of God's grace may be reflected in all their brilliance. I long to be a crystal in order to find favor in His eyes."[23]

Daily Prayer to Mary

Mary, loving daughter of God the Father, I entrust my soul to you. Protect the life of God in my soul. Do not let me lose it by sin. Protect my mind and my will so that all my thoughts and desires will be pleasing to God.

Hail Mary, full of grace, the Lord is with thee. Blessed art thou among women, and blessed is the fruit of thy womb, Jesus. Holy Mary, Mother of God, pray for us sinners, now and at the hour of our death. Amen.

Mary, loving Mother of God the Son, I entrust my heart to you. Let me love you with all my heart. Let me always try to love my neighbor. And help me avoid friends who might lead me away from Jesus and into a life of sin.

Hail Mary . . .

Mary, loving spouse of the Holy Spirit, I entrust my body to you. Let me always remember that my body is a home for the Holy Spirit who dwells in me. Let me never sin against Him by any impure actions alone or with others.

Hail Mary . . .

St. Joseph, pray for us.

St. Raphael the Archangel, pray for us.

St. Maria Goretti, pray for us.

Amen.

1   Wendy Shalit, *A Return to Modesty* (New York: Simon and Schuster, 1999), 36.

2   *New American Bible.*

3   Cf. Dannah Gresh, *Secret Keeper* (Chicago: Moody Press, 2002), 21.

4   Eric and Leslie Ludy, *When God Writes Your Love Story* (Sisters, Ore.: Loyal Publishing, 1999), 109.

5   Joyce L. Vedral, *Boyfriends: Getting Them, Keeping Them, Living Without Them* (New York: Ballantine Books, 1990), 71.

6   Cf. National Institutes of Health, "Scientific Evidence on Condom Effectiveness for Sexually Transmitted Disease (STD) Prevention" (June, 2000), 26; House of Representatives, "Breast and Cervical Cancer Prevention and Treatment Act of 1999," November 22, 1999.

7   Winer, et al., "Genital Human Papillomavirus Infection: Incidence and Risk Factors in a Cohort of Female University Students," *American Journal of Epidemiology* 157:3 (2003): 218-226; C. Sonnex, et al., "Detection of Human Papillomavirus DNA on the Fingers of Patients with Genital Warts," *Sexually Transmitted Infections* 75 (1999): 317–319

8   Dunne, et al., "Prevalence of HPV Infection Among Females in the United States," *The Journal of the American Medical Association* 297:8 (February 2007): 813-819.

9   Cf. Charles S. Morrison et al., "Hormonal Contraceptive Use, Cervical Ectopy, and the Acquisition of Cervical Infections," *Sexually Transmitted Diseases* 31, no. 9 (September 2004): 561–7; Baeten, et al., Hormonal contraception and risk of sexually transmitted disease acquisition: results from a prospective study," *American Journal of Obstetrics and Gynecology* 185:2 (August, 2001): 380-385; Blum, et al., "Antisperm Antibodies in Young Oral Contraceptive Users," *Advances in Contraception* 5 (1989): 41–46; Critchlow, et al., "Determinants of cervical ectopia and of cervicitis: age, oral contraception, specific cervical infection, smoking, and douching," *American Journal of Obstetrics and Gynecology* 173:2 (August, 1995): 534-43; Ley, et al., "Determinants of Genital Human Papillomavirus Infection in Young Women," *Journal of the National Cancer Institute* 83:14 (July, 1991): 997-1003; Prakash, et al., "Oral contraceptive use induces upregulation of the CCR5 chemokine receptor on CD4(+) T cells in the cervical epithelium of healthy women," *Journal of Reproductive Immunology* 54 (March, 2002): 117-131; Wang, et al., "Risk of HIV infection in oral contraceptive pill users: a meta-analysis," *Journal of Acquired Immune Deficiency Syndromes* 21:1 (May, 1999): 51-58; Cf. Yovel, et al., "The Effects of Sex, Menstrual Cycle, and Oral Contraceptives on the Number and Activity of Natural Killer Cells," *Gynecologic Oncology* 81:2 (May, 2001): 254-262, Lavreys, et al., "Hormonal contraception and risk of HIV-1 acquisition: results from a 10-year prospective study," *AIDS* 18:4 (March, 2004): 695-697.

10 Cf. National Institutes of Health, "Workshop Summary: Scientific Evidence on Condom Effectiveness for Sexually Transmitted Disease (STD) Prevention."

11 Shlay, et al., "Comparison of sexually transmitted disease prevalence by reported level of condom use among patients attending an urban sexually transmitted disease clinic," *Sexually Transmitted Diseases* 31:3 (2004): 154-160; Wald, et al., "The relationship between condom use and herpes simplex virus acquisition," *Annals of Internal Medicine* 143:10 (2005): 707-713.

12 American College of Obstetricians and Gynecologists, "Gynecologic Problems: Genital Herpes," December 1985.

13 Cf. Joe McIlhaney, *Safe Sex* (Grand Rapids, Mich.: Baker Books, 1992), 23.

14 Cf. Thomas Lickona, *Sex, Love and You: Study Guide* (Notre Dame, Ind.: Ave Maria Press, 2003), 14.

15 Cf. Chris Kahlenborn, MD, et al., "Oral Contraceptive Use as a Risk Factor for Premenopausal Breast Cancer: A Meta-analysis," *Mayo Clinic Proceedings* 81:10 (October, 2006): 1290-1302; Collaborative Group on Hormonal Factors in Breast Cancer, "Breast cancer and hormonal contraceptives: collaborative reanalysis of individual data on 53,297 women with breast cancer and 100,239 women without breast cancer from 54 epidemiological studies," *Lancet* 347 (June, 1996): 1713-1727; World Health Organization, "IARC Monographs Programme Finds Combined Estrogen-Progestogen Contraceptives and Menopausal Therapy are Carcinogenic to Humans," International Agency for Research on Cancer, Press Release 167 (July 29, 2005).

16 Cf. *Physicians' Desk Reference*, 2414, 2626, 2411; Larimore, et al., "Postfertilization Effects of Oral Contraceptives and Their Relationship to Informed Consent," *Archives of Family Medicine* 9 (2000): 126-133.

17 Visit www.naprotechnology.com or search the NFP Directory at www.omsoul.com .

18 Cf. Diana Russell, "The Incidence and Prevalence of Intrafamilial and Extrafamilial Sexual Abuse of Female Children," in *Handbook on Sexual Abuse of Children*, ed. Lenore Walker (New York: Springer Publishing Co., 1988).

19 John Paul II, address to the youth of Rome and Lazio, April 1, 2004.

20 John Paul II, homily at concluding Mass of World Youth Day, July 28, 2002.

21 Mother Teresa, as quoted in *Our Sunday Visitor*, September 21, 1997.

22 Fulton Sheen, *The World's First Love* (San Francisco: Ignatius, 1996), 10.

23 St. Maria Faustina Kowalska, *Diary: Divine Mercy in My Soul* (Stockbridge, Mass.: Marians of the Immaculate Conception, 2002), 318

TWENTY-FIVE LIES STAND BETWEEN ABUSE SURVIVORS AND THE HEALING THEY DESERVE.

They often believe:
It was my fault. | I'm fine. Really. | I can't tell anyone.
I'll get help later. | I'll never be healed.
I'll never trust again. | I'm unlovable. | I can't forgive.
God abandoned me…

In *Made New*, Crystalina Evert defuses the
power of these lies and others by speaking truth
into each of them, showing that no matter what
a woman has been through in life, the past
doesn't need to determine her future.

ORDER YOUR COPY AT